Wyoming

A collection of Acrostic Poems

Written and Illustrated by

Monica A. William Northrop

BookLeaf
Publishing

India | USA | UK

Wyoming © 2022 Monica A. William Northrop

Presentation by *BookLeaf Publishing*

Web: www.bookleafpub.com

E-mail: info@bookleafpub.com

ISBN : 9789358360653

First edition 2022

Childlike laughter,

Howling screams, all

In a day's adventure.

Let this be a keepsake of

       your time here;

Dear Johannes and Marion,

Raise your sights to the

       peak always,

Each experience is an

       adventure enfolding the

Next chapter life has to offer.

Acknowledgement

Picture this;

Ending the day with

some libation –

Telling tales of daily doings,

Every time it all comes crushing,

there you are, a

Rock , my rock – thank you.

Family near and far, thank you.

Preface

Pairing words and images –

Relaying what my eyes see,

Ears hear – senses galore !

For language is an art,

And so this comes to be –

Combining riddles

    and descriptions –

Enticing your imagination,

    one letter at a time.

1.

Roam free, and you'll hear
A call that at first might seem strange. Do
Not fear, for it's not the voice of a stranger -
it is the
Cry of your spirit, away from it all - finally
Home.

2.

Running along carefully -

Over and on and over,

Cutting across the first road -

Knowing that the end is just

another beginning.

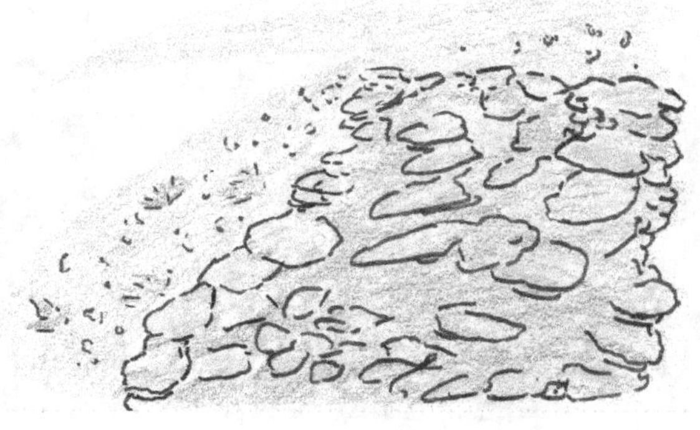

3.

Switching colors -

Alternating between brown and green,

Grass is a luxury out here -

Even in the height of daylight.

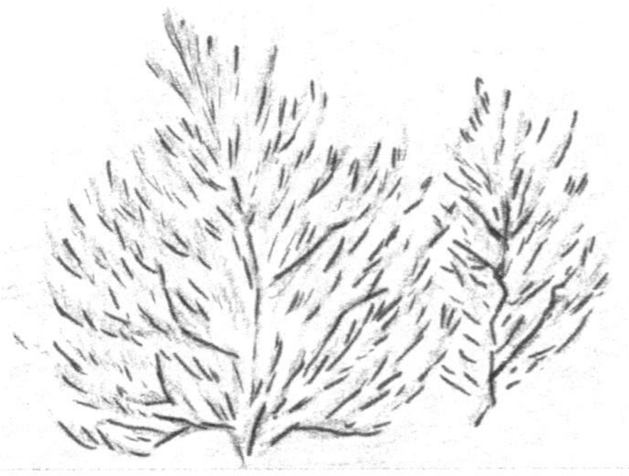

4.

Dry as a left-out bread,

Existing purely on Providence.

Searching for shade -

Eclipsed by the vast emptiness -

Reminding one of the need -

The existential crisis sans God.

5.

Sitting on the patio,

I see at a distance -

Landscapes reaching for heaven,

Entering into a daze of nothingness -

Noting the little things that matter -

Coffee, children and laughter,

Echelons of nature - no man can make.

6.

Watch out!
I lost it - there it goes -
Never leave your rug unattended, or
Draw up a plan to cross the desert in search

of it.

7.

See the calendar? -
No, you're right - it's May -
Outside in shorts and sandals ?
Welcome, crystallized waters.

8.

Caressing the high peaks gently -
Linear across the vast emptiness,
Overlooking desert and mountains alike -
Unveiling gently as the day goes by,
Delineating imaginary characters to those who

build castles in the air.

9.

Run - run if you see one!

Attempt not a knightly trait,

Tempt not your fate -

Tease not the warning you hear.

Little to no time you have!

Epic is not what you're looking for.

10.

Absolutely stoic as one,

Necessarily synchronized as a herd -

Try to catch one if you can -

Enjoying the sun and wind.

Lurk a little closer -

Oh, where they play - a

Puzzle if you will - can you discover an

Estimate of my meridian and parallel ?

11.

Endangering naught the passerby -
Looks that are complementary to their cousin -
Keeping ivories that time has left untouched.

12.

Songs of chirping voices,
Awake me almost every morning.
Good morning they say -
Eagerly awaiting my answer.
Brazen they are, these little creatures -
Rummaging through the dry, cracked earth.
Undeterred by the presence of predators -
Searching for sustenance,
Hiding among the little brushes.

See, I like these little ones -
Patio defiled or not.
After all, it is how the wildflowers grow.
Resigned to play my part in the beautification
of the high desert -
Right after my morning coffee I start,
On my patio -
Washing away doo-doos that may one day
bloom.

13.

Count them - one, two, three, four hundred -

Along the windows they come a grazing,

Tell the kids they are here,

The Nature channel is on again-

Late afternoon entertainment,

Effervescent kids and calves alike.

14.

Hovering around hay -

Observe how they observe,

Rugged yet majestic -

Strong yet gentle -

Equine aristocrats running wild.

15.

Covered in mud- mud boots - that's what

they're for !

Overnight they stay awake,

Watching over birthing cows -

Being midwives and mothers when needed,

Operating as good fathers, no less.

Yes, they are rare -

these gentlemen of the West.

16.

Big and bold -
Enormous to say the least.
A lore once was told of a bear and of a beast.
Resisting the clutch of the anonymous beast -
This bear hung on to dear life.
On the peak, it used all it had -
Overlooking the edge it took its final step.
The tooth alas is all that's left,
High up on the mountain range.

17.

Shimmering, splendid -
Thousands of suns a-blazing -
And yonder will you see,
Remnants of what once was -
Stories of the past now diamonds in the dark.

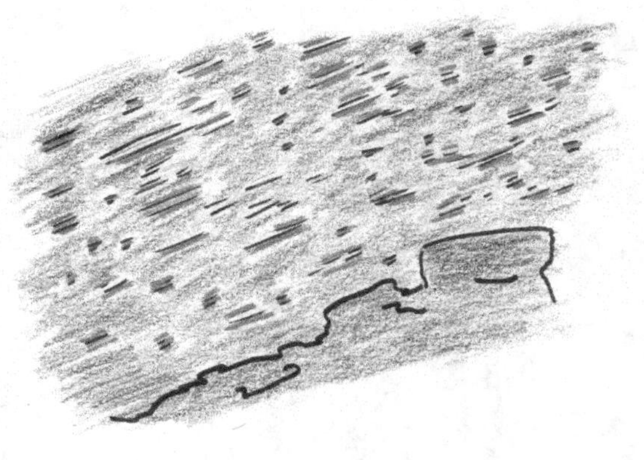

18.

Mystical glow illuminating the vast night sky,
On a clear night -
Opulent amongst the glittering stars.
Now some may say:
Look there is a man on it!
I've tried to gaze hard and yet all I see is a
Giant ball of wonder that exuberates beauty -
Heightened on a darker night than others -
The rays of light that bring hope and guidance.

19.

Venus compares not - a myth void of truth -

A lady stands demure,

Looking and watching over all creation -

Little people gather around her,

Engaging in conversation - do you know of her?

Yonder she stands demure -

    Our Lady of the Valley.

20.

Marvels of nature can't be explained -
One that Science tries hard to unravel.
Unveiling the mysteries of the world before us -
Navigates its way only to prove
            without doubt - that
There is a Maker,
And He is perfect.
In all humility and awe,
            one can only exclaim a
Never-ending Hallelujah.